# Where to find minibeasts

# In the soil

## Sarah Ridley

W

FRANKLIN WATTS

LONDON•SYDNEY

This edition 2010

Franklin Watts,
338 Euston Road,
London, NW1 3BH

Franklin Watts Australia,
Level 17/207 Kent Street,
Sydney, NSW 2000

Series editor: Sarah Peutrill
Art director: Jonathan Hair
Design: Jane Hawkins
Illustrations: John Alston

Every attempt has been made to clear copyright.
Should there be any inadvertent omission please
apply to the publisher for rectification.

Dewey number: 595.7

ISBN: 978 1 4451 0276 4

Printed in China

Franklin Watts is a division of Hachette Children's
Books, an Hachette UK company.
www.hachette.co.uk

The measures for the minibeasts in this book are typical sizes for the type of species shown in the photograph. Types within groups can vary in size enormously.

# Contents

Words in **bold** are in the glossary on pages 28–29.

 Your parent or carer may want you to wear disposable gloves or gardening gloves before you poke around in the soil.

# Under your feet

The ground under your feet is a **habitat** full of minibeasts, such as worms, millipedes and centipedes. For many minibeasts, soil is where they make their homes and find their food.

Worms can grow up to 30 cm long.

This ant can grow up to 0.4 cm long.

▲ Ants at the entrance to their nest.

▲ An earthworm tunnels up through the soil.

## What is a minibeast?

Minibeast is the name given to thousands of small animals, from bees to beetles, wasps to worms. Although many are **insects**, others are not. None of them has a **backbone**, so scientists give them the name '**invertebrate**'.

## Underground homes

Many minibeasts build their homes underground. Even small minibeasts, such as ants, can move grains of soil to make tunnels and chambers as they build a nest.

## TOP TIP!

Learn to use your eyes and you will see holes in the ground that lead to minibeast homes. Look out for more boxes like this to help you become a good minibeast spotter.

## Rubbish disposers

Several minibeasts that live in soil break down dead plant material by eating it. They **recycle** it back into the soil, where it helps plants to grow well. Without these minibeasts there would be piles of dead and **rotting** plant material in our open spaces.

▼ Slugs eat garden vegetables and also wild mushrooms and plants. They can often be seen travelling across soil in search of food.

The red slug can grow up to 18 cm long.

# Watch those holes!

A sunny bank can become home to **solitary** bees. Look out for them popping in and out of their earth holes.

## Bees all alone

Many types of bee live alone in their own **burrow**, rather than in a **hive** or **colony**. Each bee digs out a small tunnel leading to an underground chamber. Inside her hole the bee lays her eggs, which hatch into **larvae** and eventually turn into adult bees.

This bee can grow up to 1.4 cm long. ⊢——⊣

▲ If you find a hole like this, perhaps against a wall or near a path, it may be a bee nest.

▼ A bee collects plant **pollen** and **nectar** to feed to the larvae.

## TOP TIP!

Look out for bees nesting under a garden shed, in a hole in the wall or inside plant stems. These bees also live alone.

◀ The mining bee pushes the earth behind her as she burrows down into the soil to make a home for her eggs.

## Hibernating bumble

Bumble bees live in small colonies. In the autumn, the colony dies off as the weather grows cold. Only the **queen** survives, burrowing down into the soil or under some leaves. Here she drops into a deep sleep called **hibernation**. When she awakes, she crawls out, starts feeding and then finds a good place to lay her eggs and start a new colony.

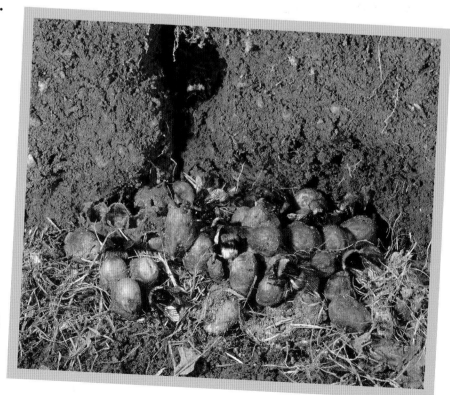

▶ This is an underground bumble bee colony.

# Underground wasps

Many wasps, like solitary bees, live alone in holes in the ground. Others live in nests containing thousands of wasps.

## Getting started

In the spring, a queen wasp searches for a good place to build a nest, such as an empty rabbit burrow. Here she builds a nest and lays some eggs. The eggs hatch into larvae that she feeds until they turn into worker wasps.

▲ A badger has damaged this wasps' nest, built inside a rabbit burrow.

## Bigger and bigger

The worker wasps build up the nest. The queen lays a large number of eggs. Other worker wasps feed the larvae hatching out from the queen's eggs.

◄ This wasps' nest has been split open to show the eggs and larvae inside.

▶ Wasps build their nests from paper. Look out for wasps on wood such as garden furniture. They collect tiny pieces of wood, mix them with **saliva** and use this mixture to build up the nest in layers.

## TOP TIP!

If you see several wasps coming and going from the same spot, you have probably found a wasps' nest. Keep your distance! Wasps will defend their nest by stinging you.

This wasp can grow up to 1.7 cm long.

# Hexagonal homes

A wasps' nest is made of six-sided (hexagonal) paper **cells**. Each cell contains one egg. The eggs hatch into hungry larvae that eventually turn into adult wasps.

◀ This close-up of the inside of a wasps' nest shows how the cells fit together.

# Mud swirls

Have you ever seen little swirls of mud on the lawn or at the park? These are worm casts, or worm poo. Worms leave them behind on the surface and then burrow back down into the soil.

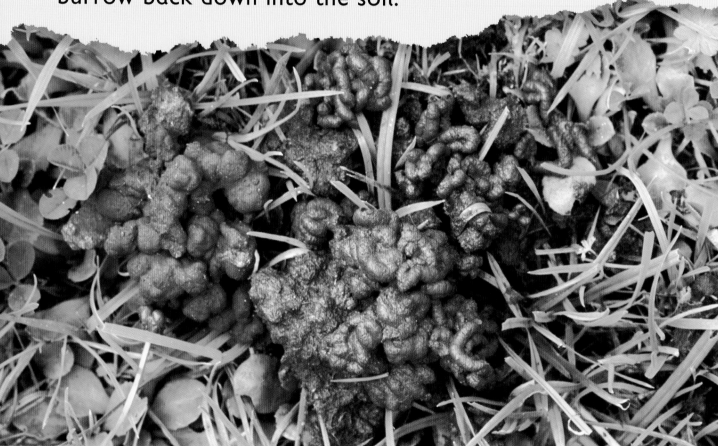

## Wiggling worms

Worms spend their lives burrowing underground. They make tunnels by pushing through the soil and eating some of it as well. Any dead plant material in the soil becomes the worms' food. The waste passes through the worms and comes out as smooth, wet soil.

▲ A worm cast does not smell – it is just a pile of soil that has passed through a worm's body.

# Head or tail?

Most worms are a pale pink colour. The head is the pointed end and the tail the flatter end. If you can't work it out, check the direction in which the worm is moving — the head will be at the front.

▲ Some people think a worm will survive if it is cut in half. It won't!

# Worm lovers

Lots of animals like to eat worms for food. Birds, hedgehogs, badgers, moles, shrews and some minibeasts think worms are tasty.

▶ Worms are good food for birds and other animals.

# Important worms

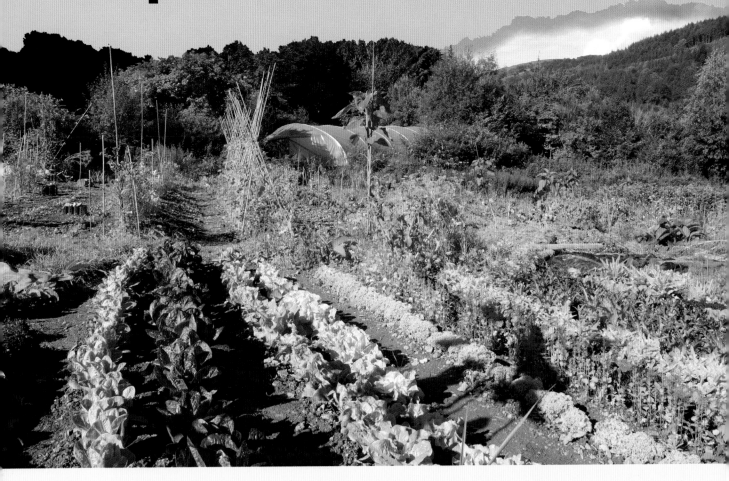

▲ Under the ground, worms will have helped these plants to grow well by mixing up the soil, making air spaces and making the soil **fertile**.

Watch how worms mix soil by making this simple wormery.

**You will need:**
- 2 jugs • Soil • Sand
- A glass jar, tank or plastic container
- 3 or 4 earthworms • A few leaves
- Black paper
- Sticky tape

## What to do:

- Fill one jug with soil, another with sand and start filling the container from these with layers of sand and soil in turn.

- Add the earthworms and some leaves.

- Wrap a black paper cover around your container and fix it on with sticky tape.

- Keep the wormery in a cool place.

- After a few days, take the black paper off to see what the worms have done to the layers.

- Remember to return the worms to where you found them as they can soon dry out and die.

# Crazy centipedes

This centipede can grow up to 3.5 cm long.

▲ A centipede has a pair of legs on each **segment**, or section, of its body.

Dig in the soil and you may see a long, pale minibeast with many legs. This is a centipede and its name means 'a hundred legs'. In fact, some centipedes have less than a hundred legs and others more.

▼ Centipedes that live in soil can tie themselves in knots!

## Dark and damp

Centipedes are **nocturnal** and like to rest in the dark, damp soil during the day. When the weather is hot and the sun dries the upper layers, centipedes burrow down to where the soil is still damp.

## TOP TIP!

To search for some centipedes, use a spade to turn over some soil in the garden. Ask an adult first! Some types of centipede live under stones or in compost heaps, so try searching for them there as well.

# Night hunters

At night, centipedes become fierce, fast **predators**. With their flat, flexible bodies, they can chase another minibeast wherever it goes – even under stones. They eat beetles, spiders, slugs, snails, worms – and each other!

▲ A centipede kills a worm by injecting it with poison.

## Caring parent

A mother centipede lays her eggs in the soil. Several types of centipede stay with their eggs and then their young until they are old enough to survive alone. When the tiny centipedes hatch out, the mother stays with them until they are old enough to survive alone.

◀ The mother centipede curls her body around the eggs while she waits for them to hatch.

17

# Munching millipedes

Millipedes push through the soil, or along the surface, searching for food. Their smooth, strong bodies help them to slide through the soil or **leaf litter**, pushed along by all those legs.

## Slow movers

Despite the name, which means 'a thousand legs', no millipede has as many as that. Millipedes do have lots of legs though – two pairs on each segment of their body.

This flat-backed millipede can grow up to 2.4 cm long.

▲ The flat-backed millipede looks a bit like a centipede.

This snake millipede can grow up to 3 cm long.

▲ This is a snake millipede. A millipede moves slowly on its short legs.

## Helpful plant-eaters

Unlike centipedes, millipedes do not need to be speedy because they eat dead plant material. They help us all by breaking down rotting or dead plants.

# Defence

When a millipede feels in danger, it curls up in a spiral. This makes it more difficult to attack. Some millipedes also squirt a bad-smelling liquid that puts many animals off eating them.

▲ The pill millipede looks very like the pill woodlouse.

### How to tell a millipede from a centipede

| MILLIPEDE: | CENTIPEDE: |
|---|---|
| slow mover | fast mover |
| two pairs of legs per segment | one pair of legs per segment |
| rounded body | flat body |
| short **antennae** | long antennae |

# Beetles and their babies

There are thousands of different types of beetle worldwide – some live in water, others in the desert and some in gardens.

## Greedy grubs

The female cockchafer beetle digs down into the soil to lay her eggs. When they hatch, the **grubs** stay underground for about two years. They feed on plant roots and can cause a lot of damage.

▶ Gardeners and farmers view cockchafer grubs as pests.

This cockchafer grub can grow up to 4.5 cm long.

**TOP TIP!**
Another place to find beetle grubs is under the bark of rotting trees. You may also see woodlice, centipedes and millipedes.

## Sexton beetles

Sexton beetles make sure their grubs will have a good supply of food when they hatch. They dig out some of the soil underneath a dead animal, such as a mouse. The body sinks down, until it is almost covered by soil. Then the beetles lay their eggs in the soil close by. When the grubs hatch, they feed on the dead animal.

This sexton beetle can grow up to 3 cm long.

▲ The adult sexton beetle also eats dead animals. It helps to speed up the rotting process.

## Terrible tiger grubs

The tiger beetle grub digs itself a pit and lurks inside. When a minibeast passes by, the grub lunges out to catch it or waits for it to fall into the pit.

▲ Look out for small, round holes in sunny spots. Can you spot the tiger beetle grubs ready to pounce?

These tiger grubs can grow up to 4.5 cm long.

# Minibeast eggs

Many minibeasts lay their eggs in the soil. Some build amazing homes for their eggs and larvae; a few protect their eggs until they hatch; others just bury their eggs in the soil and leave.

## Shiny white balls

Snails and slugs lay their shiny, white eggs in damp soil or other places where the eggs will not dry out. Depending on how warm the soil is, the eggs hatch after a few weeks.

▶ This snail has pushed its body into the soil to lay eggs.

This snail's shell can grow up to 4 cm across.

# Ant eggs

Ants live in big groups, in homes called colonies or nests. While some ants build their nest under a stone, others go down a crack in the earth and start building. Ants dig out tunnels to connect the chambers where they care for their eggs and larvae.

▲ Ant eggs are white and look like small grains of rice.

This grasshopper can grow up to 2 cm long.

▲ Grasshoppers push the tail end of their body into the soil and lay eggs close together under the ground.

# A handful of soil

To find some of the minibeasts that live in soil, follow the activity shown here.

**You will need:**

- A large sheet of white paper
- Disposable gloves
- A handful of garden soil
- A fine paintbrush
- Collecting pots or tubs
- A magnifying glass or microscope

**What to do:**

- Lay the sheet of paper on a table.
- Wearing the gloves, fetch a handful of soil.
- Carefully tip the soil onto the white paper and spread it around.
- Using the paintbrush, slowly move the soil around to look for minibeasts.
- Carefully lift the minibeasts into a collecting pot.

- The magnifying glass will help you to see things more clearly.

- Use the identification guide on pages 26–27 to help you.

- Remember to return the soil and the minibeasts to where you found them.

▼ You could repeat this activity using a handful of leaf litter. Minibeasts that live in soil are often found in leaf litter also.

▲ A magnifying glass may help you to see a pseudoscorpion. This minibeast lives in leaf litter, soil or compost.

This pseudoscorpion can grow up to 0.3 cm long.

⚠ Wash your hands after you have handled soil.

# Identification guide

Use this guide to help you identify the minibeasts that you find. They are listed in the order in which they are featured in the book. Some other common minibeasts you might come across are listed at the end. As there are thousands of different minibeasts, you may need to use a field guide or the Internet as well.

**Bee**: Bees are flying insects. Some bees live in huge, complex nests or hives; others live in holes in the ground. All bees sting if they feel they are in danger, so don't touch!

**Millipede**: A millipede is long and slim and moves slowly on its many legs. There are several different types (see pages 18–19).

**Wasp**: A flying insect with two pairs of wings. Wasps build nests underground or in roof spaces. If wasps feel they are in danger they will sting, so don't touch!

**Beetle**: An insect with two pairs of wings. The front wings have become a hard, shiny wing case to protect the soft back wings, used for flying.

**Worm**: A long, pale minibeast that spends most of its life tunnelling underground.

**Beetle grub**: The young of a beetle, also called a larva. Some grubs live underground, others in rotting wood.

**Centipede**: A fast-moving flat, long minibeast with several pairs of legs sticking out to the sides. It hunts other minibeasts.

**Snail**: The snail carries its shell on its soft body and is a **mollusc**  like the slug.

**Slug**: A mollusc, the slug has a shiny, wet body and moves along on its one 'foot'.

**Harvestman**:
A harvestman has eight legs and a body in one piece. It belongs to the arachnid family of animals, like the spider.

**Ant**: The ant is an insect and is related to wasps and bees. There are thousands of different types of ant worldwide. They build nests, also called colonies.

**Mite**: This tiny animal has eight legs and is an arachnid, like the spider.

**Slug, snail and ant eggs**: Snail and slug eggs are shiny, damp, white balls. Ant eggs are small, oval, white or yellow eggs, similar in size to a grain of rice.

**Springtail**: This tiny insect is about the size of a pin head. There are many types but they all have six legs, antennae and a special spring under their tail. This allows them to jump.

**Grasshopper**: An insect with strong back legs for jumping, as well as wings for flying.

**Spider**: Spiders come in all shapes and sizes but they all have eight legs and a body in two parts. They belong to the arachnids and are not insects.

**Pseudoscorpion**: A tiny **arachnid**, from the same minibeast family as the spider, the pseudoscorpion has large pincers at the front of its body.

**Silverfish**: Silverfish have remained almost the same since the time of the dinosaurs. These small, grey insects like dark, damp places and feed on tiny plants in the soil.

**Woodlouse**: A small, usually grey animal with a hard, armoured skin. It is a **crustacean** and lives in dark, damp places.

**Earwig**: A small, brown, shiny insect with pincers at the back of its body. It usually lives under stones or in cracks in the wall or ground.

# Glossary

**Antennae** The pair or pairs of bendy threads joined to an insect's head and used for smell, taste and touch.

**Arachnid** An animal with eight legs, like a spider, harvestman or mite.

**Backbone** The line of bones down the middle of the back.

**Burrow** An underground animal home made by digging out soil.

**Cell** In a bees' or wasps' nest, the six-sided (hexagonal) space used for an egg, larva or food.

**Colony** Many types of minibeast, including ants and wasps, live in big groups called colonies or nests.

**Crustaceans** A large group of animals, usually with a hard skin or shell, which includes woodlice, crabs and lobsters.

**Fertile** Land or soil where plants can grow successfully.

**Grub** The name given to a beetle larva.

**Habitat** A place where certain plants and animals like to live.

**Hibernation** Many animals survive cold weather by going into a deep sleep, called hibernation.

**Hive** A man-made home for bees.

**Insects** A huge group of animals. All insects have a body in three parts — the head at one end, thorax in the middle and abdomen at the end. Six legs are attached to the body and many insects have two pairs of wings.

**Invertebrates** A huge group of animals without a backbone, including insects, worms and spiders.

**Larva (plural, larvae)** The stage in the lifecycle of many insects after they hatch from eggs.

**Leaf litter** A pile of dead leaves, pieces of bark and other plant parts.

**Molluscs** A large group of animals with soft bodies. It includes slugs, snails, mussels, octopuses and oysters.

**Nectar** The sweet liquid made by flowers and eaten by many insects.

**Nocturnal** Animals that rest during the day and are active at night.

**Pollen** A fine powder made by the flower of a plant.

**Predators** Animals that eat other animals, rather than plants or dead things.

**Queen** In wasps', ants' and bees' nests, the most important female of the group who lays all the eggs.

**Recycle** To put through a process that allows used things to be reused.

**Rot** When living things die and break down – decay.

**Saliva** A watery liquid in the mouth of an animal.

**Segment** A section of something – some minibeasts have segmented bodies, meaning they are made up of many similar sections joined together.

**Solitary** Living alone, like the solitary bee.

# Websites to visit

**www.uksafari.com/creepycrawlies.htm**
A website packed with photos and information about a range of minibeasts.

**www.oum.ox.ac.uk/thezone/index.htm**
The Oxford University Museum of Natural History website has an Instant ID site to help you identify minibeasts.

# Index